Psychosis of Sanity

MacKara McKenzie

Presentation by *BookLeaf Publishing*

Web: www.bookleafpub.com

E-mail: info@bookleafpub.com

ISBN: 9789357443067

First edition 2023

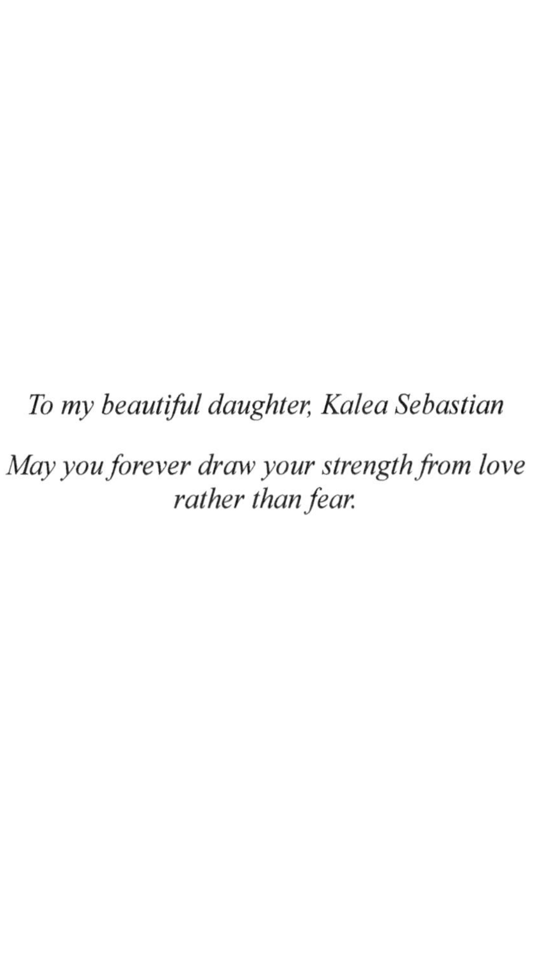

To my beautiful daughter, Kalea Sebastian

May you forever draw your strength from love
rather than fear.

ACKNOWLEDGEMENT

I would first like to acknowledge BookLeaf Publishing for the incredible opportunity that has allowed me to get my writing out in the world, bringing me one step closer to supporting others with my story.

I would also like to acknowledge my family that continually supports me in my dreams and for giving me a solid foundation on which I was raised. Without that, my life could have easily gone a very different way, but with them I have always remained firm and found ways to turn my heartaches into my greatest strengths.

Lastly, I would like to acknowledge my fiancé and father of my child, Ikeka Sebastian. In a world where I feel unseen, misunderstood, and unloved, you create a safe haven. A place in which I feel no need to hide my true self. In every way, you see me, you love me, and you support me. For that, I am forever thankful.

PREFACE

I have never been viewed as a positive person. In fact, on many occasions I have been called emotionless and pessimistic. However, the reality is that I have never had an easy time expressing any emotion other than contempt, anger, and irritation. I despise that I am unable to express all the wonderful things under the surface, making it practically impossible to connect with other human beings. It's unbearably lonely and I spend most days feeling incredibly misunderstood and unseen for who I really am.

One of my greatest goals in life is to do everything in my power to make sure other people do not feel just as misunderstood and unseen as I do. I want my readers to know that they are not alone in their struggles. Some days, I feel like a superhero: capable of doing the impossible. Other days, I feel the weight of the world crushing me and the best I can do is bare minimum. And that is okay! I hope that by allowing others a peak into my everyday struggles, it will help them to understand that giving your all will look different every day.

These poems are inspired by my daily joys, struggles, accomplishments, and (sometimes) breakdowns. I will also delve into how my past trauma and current mental states can seriously affect my every day life. I draw inspiration for these poems from each and every aspect of my life: the good, the bad, and the ugly.

Prison Cell Eyes

I drown in an unending pool of tears
Just below the surface of the eyes I have barred
up like a prison cell.
I suffocate on my own screams,
Desperately clutching at the bars,
Craving a moment of peace from my despair.
I destroy my own mind in my attempts to break
free,
There is no escape from this psychological
prison
That I have constructed for myself.

I grow wearier every day
Resisting the demons that desperately want to
destroy me
I will laugh and joke and make others smile.
As my face wrinkles with age,
My smile lines will be my defining features.
When I am thought of,
I am only remembered by my laughter.
My happiness is all I allow to shine through
This overwhelming darkness.

But it's these eyes:
They could deceive me at any moment;

All it takes is one single person.
A single person that might see through these
smiles,
The one that will look into my eyes and see the
truth.
What once were mighty lakes of blue gleaming
inside my skull,
Are now fading into a lonely sky of gray before
a rainstorm.
I am saddled with the burdensome task of
Keeping these unbearable clouds from pouring
down
allowing my true inner self to burst for all to see.

I am courageous and devoted and
compassionate,
And I will forever have a smile on my face.
This is the part of my soul I will allow others to
hold in their hearts.
I will ensure the demons I hold hostage
Behind my faded, prison cell eyes
Never make an appearance.
This is what I want.

I need this.
I want this.
Do I want this?
Is that to be my life from now until always?
Cowering behind a façade?

Nothing but masks of laughs and smiles?

Yes.
This is what I must do.
Until the right person can see my true self,
Look into my eyes and just notice.
Convince me that my demons are to be
embraced
Rather than feared.
How tremendous it would be
To not hide the other half of myself.
But who's to say that day will ever come?
Until then, I will continue on as I have.
I will bathe in the salt water oceans with no
escape
For however long I must,
Until someone comes along
With the keys to my cell.
Until then. Until that day. I will carry on.

I Find My Comfort Here

My body,
Heavy with exhaustion,
Falling in slow motion,
Sinking into our bed,
Looking for comfort.
From back to side I roll
To meet your body
My fingers slow dance along your side
My head finds its home on your chest
Your heartbeat sings in my ear

There before me lies an eyelash,
My eyelash,
Fallen from me.
That tiny piece my body gifted to you
At that moment.
All the tears that have graced that single eyelash,
Every heartache that it bears
Lie on your chest.
Rising and falling with every breath
As if it had been plucked straight from the lungs
inside you.

Clings to you
Like the heart you keep glued to your sleeve.

The eyelash falls away;
Damp mascara leaves a stain
Imprinted on your skin.
A gift
Given to you
To hold in your heart.
One piece,
A thousand tears

Ode to My Daughter

A seed planted within me, given unknowingly,
Blossoming inside my opulent womb much
Like a sprout out of moist, fertilized soil.
Greatness emanates from this seedling bestowed
upon me.
I marvel at the growth and choose to trust
That every ache, pain, and mark on my body
Is nothing compared to this extraordinary love.
My heartbeat is your life support; my body, your
home.
I give my body so you can grow to be
Strong enough to grow alone, for one day you
must.

The first part of our journey together ends as
they place you on my chest.
We both scream a tearful farewell; it is a
bittersweet goodbye.
Our story still continues, for we only closed the
first chapter.
This beauty I carried-I now see her grow with
each day. I'm blessed.
I water her with my love and guidance and I
stand by

As she learns to grow alone, while I can still be right next
To her to catch her when she falls. I will be right by her side.
This body may no longer be her home, but these hands can be her safety net
For as long as she needs me, I will do my best.
My beautiful flower should never feel afraid to try.

The time will come that my dear child no longer needs my guidance.
She will have grown strong enough to stand alone
It will be her turn-just as it was mine-to not only grow, but blossom.
After years of devotion, tears, laughter, and defiance;
How I spent that time with her will set the tone
For the future steps she takes in her own dance.
With every brick she is thrown,
Will she use those bricks to build herself a safe haven
Or bury herself in the heavy abundance?
I will have to let go, for that life will be hers alone.

Mom Guilt

Someone asks me,
"Do you ever miss the before?"
The before stretch marks,
The before aches and pains,
The before saying the same thing again and
again?
The before dirty diapers,
The before tantrums,
The before using every ounce of your energy
and then some?
Well, of course not!
The greatest gift a woman could get, I've got.

Scars on my skin, purple and hideous
My body, this vessel, now always feels pain
It was just part of the beautiful experience,
Why would I complain?
Repetition will keep me sharp
It doesn't matter that I've said it sixteen times
In the grand scheme, it's just one little part
It's okay, I'm fine.

Wiping up the dirty butt,
Comforting her as she screams.
Loving her no matter what

And getting to fulfill her needs.
I have energy for the sole purpose
Of keeping her smiling
All day, chasing her around the house
Why would I need any for me?

This body, it grew her.
This voice, it teaches her.
These hands, they hold her.
This life, it leads her.
I am so she can be
But then someone asks me,
"Do you ever miss the before?"
Every day.
Maybe just a little bit more
Than what's okay.

Unheard Desperation

Drowning
I'm drowning.
Drowning in trying
Drowning in failing
Drowning in tears
Drowning in fear
Drowning in desperation

Please,
I need help.
Please, take my hand
Please, pull me out
Please, tell me I can
Please, help me swim
Please, don't let me drown

Why?
Can't you hear my cries?
Why can't you notice?
Why can't you hear my voice?
Why am I screaming when there is no point?
Why do I keep slipping back?
Why can't I stop drowning?

Drowning, I keep drowning.
Please, I still need help.
Why can't you hear my cries?
I can't stop drowning.
I can't stop screaming.
And you can't hear me.
So I drown, unheard and alone.

I Will Be That Voice

One day I
Will make a difference.
I can be the voice
Of someone with no words.
I can make the choice
To inspire those
With no hope,
Because if I chose
To be there
For the ones for which it's just not fair:
The kids with no family,
The people with no homes,
The ones who feel all alone.
I can be the change
I want to see in the world.
I can rearrange
The broken pieces
In all the people
That just need a voice.
I will make that choice,
And I will be that voice.
And my voice will be the one,
No matter how small,
Will make the change for all.

Sestina of the Boy and the Girl

From across the room, the girl admires the
handsome boy.
He looks up to notice the smitten girl,
And she throws him a nervous smile.
Oh, how the girl harbored such a grave
Desire to be that boy's love.
When the boy approached, her anxiety brought
her to tears.

The girl used her sleeve to wipe the tears
As she found the courage to say hello to the boy.
One conversation, and she fell in love.
Yes, this is the story of a girl
Who fell too quickly into her grave
Of heartbreak. Through it, she tries to smile.

The girl couldn't help but stare at the boy's
smile;
It convinced her he would never cause her tears.
They promised to take each other's secrets to the
grave
So the girl entrusted her mind to the boy.
He sacrificed his needs to protect the girl.
The two relished in their season of young love.

Conflict is inevitable in the game of love.
The girl told the boy she had run out of her
smile.
Deep was the inner pain felt by the girl.
Her nights were spent drowning in her tears.
That burden became too heavy; she wanted to
say goodbye to the boy.
He told the girl he refuses to stand over her
grave.

Young love with heavy burdens did come with
grave
Consequences. It became hard to stay in love.
The girl still cared immensely for the boy,
But he seemed to have also lost his smile.
A decision was made that caused many tears;
Their young love had died and so did the dream
of the girl.

It was a difficult day for the girl.
She found herself placing flowers on a grave,
Failing to fight the flooding tears.
She never could let go of that first love;
She will never forget that handsome smile.
For one last time, she says goodbye to the boy.

She stops fighting the tears, so she can mourn her love.
She thought she would be the girl who laid in a grave.
Across her face lies a broken smile, as she forever carries the heart of the boy.

I See You

I see you in
The movie theater gives me anxiety.
Too many people,
Always having to wait in a line,
That uncomfortable moment
Having to squeeze past a row of people
To get to your seat.
But there was a time
When it was a good kind of anxiety.
The butterflies in my stomach, anxiety.
Sitting with you
In the back row, anxiety.
Holding hands and throwing candy in the air
Trying to catch it with our mouths, anxiety.
My first crush.
I didn't know how amazing it would end up
becoming.
I still remember how my little girl heart fluttered
Sitting there with you in the movie theater.

I see you in
Christmas Eve is such a joyful night.
Spending time with the family,
Opening Christmas Eve pajamas,
Watching Christmas movies all night.

The excitement of seeing
Presents under the tree,
Trying to guess
What you will be unwrapping
The very next morning.
I remember my Christmas Eve last year.
I visited you.
Just to say Merry Christmas
And leave flowers on your grave.
It was the first Christmas
With you gone.

I see you in
The stars are so interesting,
Don't you think?
A sky full of pitch black and
You look up to see
What seems to be
These tiny openings in the heavens;
Shining all night for us
Like our lost loved ones
Trying to be our nightlights.
Because deep down we are all
Little kids-still scared of the dark.
So when the night comes,
I look for the brightest star
And I know it's you shining for me.
My night light.

I see you in
Everything.
Everywhere.
I see you.
Only it's not you.
It's just memories of you.
But for now,
I will find happiness in that,
Until the day
When I take my last breath
And go home.
When I can really see you.
Until then,
I thank you for all the wonderful memories,
The moments that keep me happy, even now,
Even in the darkness.
Thank you for being my nightlight.
So I will be outside
Talking to the stars.
Because that is where
I see you.

"I Love You Up To The Sky and Back"

"I love you up to the sky and back"
Anger arose when I heard those words
Slicing through my beating heart like swords
"I love you up to the sky and back"
That phrase is nothing more than a lie.
Please, please just tell me why;
Why would you take such a beautiful saying
And make it something I fear to hear?

"I love you up to the sky and back"
Where were you to prove that in the past?
Can't prove it now that you've gone too fast.
You are one with the heavens,
No longer with the earth;
I never knew what you could've been worth
Until you were gone.

"I love you up to the sky and back"
Sadness wells up to these faded eyes
And I watch the tears fall to the floor
Nothing is important anymore
I can hear through my sorrow filled sighs
Your voice in the back of my mind,
"I love you up to the sky and back"

The ability to forgive you, I still lack.
I am still so angry
Even more now
I don't know why or how.

"I love you up to the sky and back"
Love does not leave
Yet it seems you did
"I love you up to the sky and back"
I hate that.

Those Hands

My memories are like fading dreams
One moment, I hold the whole story in my hand
The next, it melts away leaving only small bits;
Leaving me with but a single detail to cherish.

I can't find entire stories in my mind with my
mother;
All I have are tiny moments, nothing else
surrounding it.
I don't remember the exact events that led her
hand to me
But, by some misfortune, I can still remember
those hands.

I remember her hands every time I brush my
hair.
The hands that made me a doll, pretty and
submissive,
Like any good girl. But if I said no;
I remember those hands pulling at my roots: I
don't get to say no.

I remember her hands every time I take a
shower.
The hands that pounded on bathroom doors
while I hid in the water,
Her man-friend outside yelling through the
bathroom window.
I remember those hands pointing and laughing
as I walked out scared.

I remember her hands every time I breathe.
The hands that despised my lack of compliance;
My resolution to defend against her would not
be tolerated.
I remember those hands squeezing the defiance
out through my neck.

I struggle to recollect the specifics, the reasons,
the circumstance,
But, boy, do I remember those hands.
Those big, grown-up, adult with all the power
hands
And feeling like nothing in the face of them.

Now here I am, holding my daughter in my
arms,
She reaches her tiny hand towards me and
grasps my finger.
I see my hands; my hands that are now those
hands.

Those big, grown-up, adult with all the power
hands.

I will use these powerful hands in a way I never
knew:
I will hold her when she is scared; I will not be
what she fears.
I will wipe away her tears; I will not be the
cause for them.
I will lift her up to reach her goals; I will not be
the weight that pulls her down.

I will be the mother my little girl deserves.
From the moment she took her first breath,
Her entire life was put into these hands.
Every day that I breathe, I will fight to be
worthy of that.

Love and Hate

24

Love and hate:
Such a fine line between the two.
There is truth
Behind this saying
Or, at least,
That's been my experience.

This is, in fact,
A tragic love story.
But not that of a boy,
Who stole my heart
Then broke it in half,
No, no.
This a story of the woman,
Who made this heart
And shattered it.

For me,
That fine line
Between love and hate,
Is the threshold between my hallway
And the bathroom.
My issue is not with the room itself,
But that of which
It has meant for me

In my life.

My counter.
This is where
I look in the mirror.
I no longer recognize the reflection
Staring back at me,
Yet,
It is so familiar.
Blonde hair,
Blue eyes,
Pale skin:
I see her
In me.

Her beauty,
It is something I've envied
For so long.
Our physical resemblance
However,
Only reminds me
That I am like her.
And soon, I fear,
My reflection may not be
The only thing about me
That is like her.

That is nothing
Compared to the shower.

The place
Where I once slipped away
To hide from her hands
And her words.
Safe and sound,
In my steam-filled hideaway.
No longer in danger
But still,
To this day,
I always find myself back there.

But of course,
What better place for privacy?
The sound of the water
Shooting from the head,
Drowning out the sounds
Of my weakness.
So I can allow myself
To cry.
To let these tears,
Overflowing with all my sorrows
And all my pain,
Flow from these dim eyes,
And trickle down my face
Until, finally,
They fall.
Down the drain,
Never to be seen again.
The warm water

It wraps itself around me
Filling the place of the person
That I wish were holding me.

So,
You see,
How could I love the place
Where I allow myself to be weak?
The place
Where I feel
So much pain?
But how could I hate it
If it is my escape from reality?
The safehouse
That keeps my secrets,
And holds my pain
Deep within its drains?
And how could I love the woman
Who hurt me?
Who left my heart
In shattered pieces
On the floor?
Who left me
For good?
But how could I hate her,
The one who gave me life?
The one who made me
As strong as I am today?
The one who died

Wanting only my forgiveness.
Love and hate:
Such a fine line between the two.

The Reality of My Nightmares

Some days I can't tell the difference between my
nightmares and reality.
I dream of unexplainable evil then wake up in a
cold sweat,
Tears rolling down my face and it is
Pitch. Black.
I live in a world where that exact same evil
wears a crown of wickedness
And roams the earth as if he is the mighty king.
He gets inside the minds of the innocent and
twists their hopes and dreams
Into endless fear.
He is uninvited and unwanted, yet he still
slithers his way into people's lives,
destroying them simply because he wants to.
He gives life to our inner demons in hopes that
they will tear us apart,
Piece by piece.
He brings death to good people because he is
terrified
At the mere thought of someone
Who might shed even the slightest bit of light on
this earth
That he has made so dark.

He uses our grief to morph us into lost souls;
He takes down whatever is good because it is a
threat to his very existence.
Evil is a vile creature that will stop at nothing
To make us feel pain words can't describe.
We can never "get over" that pain;
We can only get through it.
Day by day. Moment by moment.
And we cannot stop Evil for it is inevitable.
But we can control whether or not it takes hold
of our own lives.
So when you're having a nightmare and you
wake up in a cold sweat,
Tears rolling down your face and it is
Pitch. Black...
Just remember to turn on the light.

Alone

Room full of people.
Known them for years,
Yet they seem like strangers.
Room full of people.
But I still feel alone

So much love.
Surrounded by family.
Surrounded by friends.
So much love.
But I still feel alone.

World of opportunities.
Everything I could ever want.
All within my reach.
World of opportunities.
But I still feel alone.

No matter how many people,
No matter how much love,
No matter the opportunities,
I could have it all,
But I still feel alone.

It is a sickness;
A sickness of the mind.
So many don't understand this.
I try and I try,
But I still feel alone.

Loneliness enjoys my company.
I can never get any rest
With this unwanted guest
Constantly reminding me,
I am alone.

The Storm Before the Rainbow

Red running down my legs,
Anguished over this loss of a part of me.
I held my head in my hands
Not knowing where to go from this point,
Blood and tears plummeting to the floor.
Off the floor and staring at my heartbreak in the
mirror;
Where do I go from here?

Magic Monotony

34

I live the same life every day
Stuck in this never-ending cycle.
Yesterday and tomorrow is today,
With no escape from this monotony.
Only living my life halfway.
I am suffocated by these same four walls closing
in,
Can't even find a hideaway.
My mind is spinning as I slide down this spiral;
I don't know if I'm okay.

In the Course of a Day

Flowers, bright as a thousand suns
Surround the clear water as it runs
Through the woods and down the hill;
The gleaming lake, it does fill.
In the reflection on the water you can see
A monstrous mountain as high as can be.
If at the top of the mountain
I were to stand,
The clouds I could touch
With my very own hand.
Feel as they slowly drift by,
And watch as the sun sets in the sky.
The shining day turns into a dark night,
But the moon and the stars
Still shed some light.
As the stars glimmer millions of miles away,
I get to sit and watch as the night
Once again turns to day.

I Don't Want to Kill Myself
As Much Anymore

I don't want to kill myself as much anymore.
Sure, the idea of a release from such constant
sorrow;
It is still an appeal, just not as much as before.
There is more now: a reason to see tomorrow.

The pitter-patter of my little girl's feet brings me
joy.
Her laugh-it fills my heart.
I chuckle as she shares her snacks for the dog to
enjoy.
The idea of leaving her is unfathomable; it
would tear her life apart.

His love is more than enough reason to stay.
Nothing feels broken when he wraps me in his
embrace,
He knows how to make me feel okay.
And more than that, every day he puts a smile on
my face.

They drive me crazy in the best and worst ways.
My life stands firm in the foundation they have
built for me.

They support me in both good and bad days.
I've never had to doubt that they love me fully.

I can find happiness in myself right now.
Usually my burden carried is much more
But for today, this feeling I welcome and allow.
I don't want to kill myself as much anymore.

Enchanted by You

Every day with you, my love,
I am under your spell.
Every exquisite part of you,
I feel so enchanted.
But your mind remains blinded
By your misguided insecurities.

You see dreary, passionless eyes;
I see a pool of smooth whiskey
Reflecting sunlight through its glass.
Sacred stones of amber inside your skull.
The streams of sap from a maple tree:
A sweet entrance into your soul.

You see an unruly head of hair;
I see a quill dipped in ink
Composing a story atop your head.
Unique like a jet black dahlia
And soft like a raven's feathers.
Perfect to run my fingers through.

You see a broken smile, one meant to be hidden;
I see a blush tinted gateway from which
Your captivating laughter breaks free from your
lungs,

Moistened with an inviting, sweet dew.
A set of lips destined to embrace my own.
I am enchanted by you, my love.

www.ingramcontent.com/pod-product-compliance
Lightning Source LLC
LaVergne TN
LVHW021312200726

843509LV00012B/1883